The Heinemann Illustrated Encyclopedia

Volume 3

Cos-Eur

First published in Great Britain by Heinemann Library
Halley Court, Jordan Hill, Oxford OX2 8EJ
a division of Reed Educational and Professional Publishing Ltd.

OXFORD MELBOURNE AUCKLAND
JOHANNESBURG BLANTYRE GABORONE
IBADAN PORTSMOUTH NH (USA) CHICAGO

Series Editors: Rebecca and Stephen Vickers
Author Team: Rob Alcraft, Catherine Chambers, Jim Drake,
Fred Martin, Angela Royston, Jane Shuter, Roger Thomas,
Rebecca Vickers, Stephen Vickers
Reading Consultant: Betty Root

Photo research by Katharine Smith
Designed and Typeset by Gecko Ltd
Printed in Hong Kong by Wing King Tong

02 01 00 99 98
10 9 8 7 6 5 4 3 2 1

ISBN 0 431 09054 8

British Library Cataloguing in Publication Data.

The Heinemann illustrated encyclopedia
   1. Children's encyclopedias and dictionaries
   I. Vickers, Rebecca II. Vickers, Stephen, 1951–
032

ISBN 0431090629

Acknowledgements:
Cover: The cover illustration is of a male specimen of *Ornithoptera goliath*, commonly called
the Goliath Birdwing. Special thanks to Dr George C. McGavin and the Hope Entomological Collections,
Oxford University Museum of Natural History.

J. Allan Cash Ltd: pp4, 8, 13, 19, 34, 47. **Ardea London Ltd:** p23t. **Bruce Coleman:** Jane Burton – p11; Jorg
and Petra Wegner – p30; Konrad Wothe – p43t. **Des Conway:** p14t. **Empics:** p48; Gail Devers – 44. **FLPA/
Marineland:** p23b. **Sally and Richard Greenhill Photo Library:** Sally Greenhill – p46. **GSF Picture Library:**
p21. **The Hutchison Library:** p37; Sarah Errington – p18; Robert Francis – p39; Christine Pemberton – p12; B.
Regent – p24. **Kobal Collection:** Merrick Morton – p26b. **Oxford Scientific Films:** p25; Bob Bennett – p5b;
Mike Brown – p32t; Densey Clyne – p42b; Martin Colbeck – p41; John Cooke – p6b; Daniel J. Cox – pp5t, 16t;
Mark Deeble and Victoria Stone – p36b; Warren Faidley – p32b; David Fleetham – p42t; Jose Luis Grande – p29b;
C.W. Helliwell – p43b; Tim Jackson – p15; Jeffrey Lang – p9b; Tom Leach – p29t; Zig Leszczynski – p28;
C.C. Lockwood – p17t; John McCammon – p10t; Margaret Miller – p22b; John Mitchell – p33t; Robert Pearcy –
p22t; Leonard Lee Rue III – p16b; Roger Sackman – p35; Kjell Sandved – p6t; Tim Shepard – p33b; John Tilford –
p7t; Robert A Tyrrell – p36t; Tom Ulrich – pp9t, 10b; Fred Whitehead – p7b. **Performing Arts Library:** Colin
Willoughbey – p26t. **Redferns:** Simon King – p14b. **Rex Features:** p27t. **Science Photo Library:** p17b;
J. Knighton – p31; Peter Menzel – p40l; David Parker – p40r; Geoff Tompkinson – p27b. **Tony Stone Worldwide:**
Gavin Hellier – p38; Hugh Sitton – p20. **Trip:** Joseph Okwesa – p45.

Every effort has been made to contact copyright holders of any material
reproduced in this book. Any omissions will be rectified in subsequent printings
if notice is given to the Publisher.

Welcome to the
Heinemann Illustrated Encyclopedia

What is an encyclopedia?

An encyclopedia is an information book. It gives the most important facts about a lot of different subjects. This encyclopedia has been specially written for children your age. It covers many of the subjects from school and others you may find interesting.

What is in this encyclopedia?

In this encyclopedia each topic is called an entry. There is one page for every entry. The entries in this encyclopedia are on:

- animals
- plants
- dinosaurs
- countries
- geography
- history
- world religions
- music
- art
- transport
- science
- technology

How to use this encyclopedia

This encyclopedia has eleven books, called volumes. The first ten volumes contain entries. The entries are all in alphabetical order. This means that Volume One starts with entries that begin with the letter 'A' and Volume Ten ends with entries that begin with the letter 'Z'. Volume Eleven is the index volume and has some other interesting information in its Fact Finder section.

Here are two entries, showing you what you can find on a page:

The See also line tells you where to find other related information.

This is the letter that the entry starts with.

Fact boxes give you details about the topic.

Did You Know? boxes have fun or interesting bits of information.

The Fact File tells you important facts and figures.

Costa Rica

See also: North America

Costa Rica is a small country in Central America. It has two coasts. On the east coast it is hot and wet. On the west coast it is cooler and drier.

Living and working

Costa Rica is very green and has beautiful forests. Some people work with tourists who come to see the forests. Many Costa Ricans have small farms. Some farmers use ox carts, which they paint bright colours. Beans, coffee and maize are grown. The Costa Ricans eat beans for most meals. They also eat fried or boiled plantains.

In the towns, friends meet in cafés and sing and play the guitar. People dance to calypso and reggae music.

Bananas from Costa Rica are sold all over the world.

DID YOU KNOW?

The Costa Rican volcanoes, Mount Poás and Mount Irazu, rumble and steam. No one knows when they will next erupt.

NORTH AMERICA

FACT FILE

PEOPLE .... Costa Ricans

POPULATION .... 3.3 million

MAIN LANGUAGE .... Spanish

CAPITAL CITY .... San José

MONEY .... Colón

HIGHEST MOUNTAIN... Chirripó-Grande – 3837 m

LONGEST RIVER .... Rio Grande – 3016 km

Coyote

See also: Dog, Mammal, Wolf

The coyote is a kind of wild dog. It is a mammal. The coyote lives in the open grassland areas of North America. It is also called the prairie wolf and the brush wolf.

Coyote families

A male coyote is called a dog and a female coyote is called a bitch. Their babies are called pups, and about six are born at a time. Coyotes live in small family groups called packs. The pups are born in a cave or in a burrow called a den. Both parents feed and take care of the pups.

Thick fur keeps the coyote warm in the cold winters

A coyote

COYOTE FACTS

NUMBER OF KINDS......	1
COLOUR.......	grey and beige
LENGTH........	75–100 cm, not including tail
HEIGHT	45–55 cm
WEIGHT	up to 20 kg
STATUS	common
LIFE SPAN......	about 4 years
ENEMIES	people

A coyote's high, loud howl can be heard by other coyotes

Sharp teeth for ripping meat

Claws for digging

These are four-week-old cubs. They spend a lot of time in their den.

FOOD

Coyotes hunt at night for rabbits, ground squirrels and other small rodents. A small group of coyotes can kill a deer.

Crab

See also: Crustacean, Sea life

A crab is a crustacean with a hard shell and strong pincers. Most crabs live in seawater, often close to the shore. Some crabs live in fresh water and others live on land.

Crab families

A young crab is called a larva. The larva hatches out of an egg. As the young larva grows bigger, it has to shed its shell several times before it becomes an adult crab. Some crabs live in burrows they dig in the sand. Others hide in cracks in the rocks.

CRAB FACTS

NUMBER OF KINDS	4500
COLOUR	brown to red or yellow
LENGTH	1.5 mm–3.5 m
WEIGHT	up to 9 kg
STATUS	common
LIFE SPAN	up to 12 years
ENEMIES	squid, seabirds people

Strong claws with pincers for crushing food and attacking enemies

A land crab

Hard shell protects the body and legs

Back legs are flat paddles, for swimming through the water

This female shore crab lays many eggs at a time.

FOOD

Many shore crabs lie in wait at the entrance to their burrows. When a young turtle or lobster passes by, the crab grabs it and pulls it into its burrow to eat it. Crabs also hunt for worms and small fish.

Crane

See also: Bird

A crane is a large bird with a long neck, a long bill, long legs and long wings. Cranes live in all the continents, except for Antarctica and South America. They live in marshes and migrate to warmer places for the winter.

Crane families

Unlike most birds, male and female cranes look the same. They dance together and then build a nest, usually in marshy ground. The female lays two eggs. Both parents take turns sitting on them until they hatch. The babies leave the nest as soon as they hatch. When the chicks are strong enough, the family joins other cranes in a group called a flock.

CRANE FACTS

NUMBER OF KINDS......	14
COLOUR.......	mostly grey, black and white
HEIGHT	up to 1.6 m
WEIGHT	up to 8 kg
STATUS	some types are endangered
LIFE SPAN......	around 20 years
ENEMIES	Marshes are being drained for farmland, so cranes have fewer places to breed and find food.

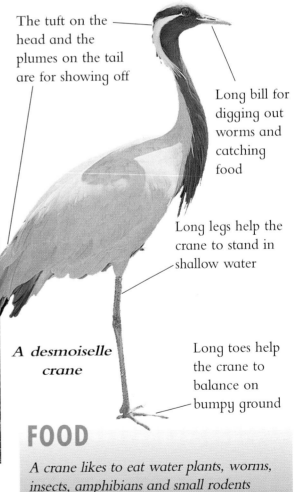

The tuft on the head and the plumes on the tail are for showing off

Long bill for digging out worms and catching food

Long legs help the crane to stand in shallow water

A desmoiselle crane

Long toes help the crane to balance on bumpy ground

This female Florida sandhill crane is waiting for her second egg to hatch.

FOOD

A crane likes to eat water plants, worms, insects, amphibians and small rodents found in the marshes.

Croatia

See also: Yugoslavia

Croatia is in south-east Europe. There are mountains and hills. The coast in the west has hot summers and cool, wet winters. It is colder inland in the winter.

Living and working

About half the Croatians live in ancient cities and towns. Half live in the countryside. People eat different foods in different parts of the country. *Brodet* is eaten by people living near the coast. It is fish cooked with olive oil and served with rice, vegetables and mushrooms. People who live inland eat a stew of beans and fresh maize.

People work in factories, farms and mines. Farmers grow cotton, tobacco, fruit and olive trees and cereal crops.

The huge wall that used to protect the old town of Dubrovnik is still standing today.

DID YOU KNOW?

Dubrovnik is an ancient, walled town on the Mediterranean coast of Croatia. It was an important port in the past. Now, many tourists visit Dubrovnik.

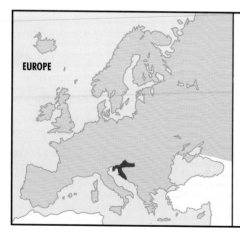

EUROPE

FACT FILE

PEOPLE	Croatians, Croats
POPULATION	4.5 million
MAIN LANGUAGE	Croatian
CAPITAL CITY	Zagreb
MONEY	Kuna
HIGHEST MOUNTAIN	Velebit Planina – 1758 m
LONGEST RIVER	River Sava – 940 km

Crocodile

See also: Alligator, Reptile

The crocodile is a very big reptile which lives in rivers and lakes. It lives in warm places in parts of Africa, North America, Australia and India. It is a close relative of the alligator, but crocodiles have more pointed snouts. Also, when a crocodile closes its jaws, its teeth still show. A crocodile can attack and kill animals, fish and people.

CROCODILE FACTS

NUMBER OF KINDS....12	
COLOUR....	greenish-brown
LENGTH.....	up to 5.5 m
WEIGHT.....	up to 700 kg
STATUS.......	American crocodile is endangered
LIFE SPAN...	up to 100 years
ENEMIES.....	Birds and lizards eat crocodile eggs. People kill crocodiles for their skin.

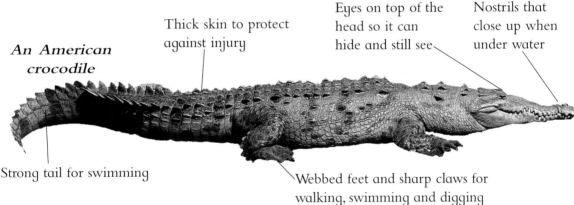

An American crocodile

Thick skin to protect against injury

Eyes on top of the head so it can hide and still see

Nostrils that close up when under water

Strong tail for swimming

Webbed feet and sharp claws for walking, swimming and digging

A hatchling has an egg tooth on the end of its snout. It uses this to pierce the egg's thick skin.

Crocodile families

Crocodile babies are called hatchlings. The mother crocodile digs a nest in the sandy shore and lays about 60 eggs. Three months later the eggs hatch. The mother takes the hatchlings gently in her mouth and carries them to the lake or river.

FOOD

Crocodiles will eat almost any animal. A big crocodile only needs to eat one or two large animals each year.

Crop

See also: Farming

Crops are plants that are grown to give people food, or other things they need, like cotton. In some countries, farmers grow crops to provide for themselves and their families. Other farmers grow crops to sell for money.

Different crops

There are many different kinds of crop. Maize, rice and wheat are called cereal crops. Fruits and vegetables are also grown as crops. Some crops are not used for food. Cotton and flax are crops grown to be made into cloth.

DID YOU KNOW?

Maize crops can be turned into a kind of fuel to power cars and trucks.

Farmers still need to check some crops by hand, like this cotton growing in Australia, to make sure there are no pests or diseases.

Caring for crops

Each kind of crop needs special care. Some crops may need extra plant food called fertilizer to help them grow. Other crops need lots of water. Rice, for example, is grown in specially flooded fields. Farmers use fences, scarecrows and chemical sprays to protect crops from animals and insects. When a crop is fully grown it has to be picked, cut down or dug up. This is called harvesting.

Plants like tomatoes can be grown in large fields as crops.

Crustacean

See also: Animal, Sea life

Crustaceans are animals with soft bodies and hard shells. They are invertebrates. As crustaceans grow bigger they shed their shells. Then, they have to hide until their larger, new shell hardens.

These freshwater shrimps swim in and out of a crack in a rock.

Crustacean families

All crustaceans lay eggs. Some, like the shore crab, carry the eggs until they hatch. Others leave the eggs to hatch by themselves. The eggs hatch as tiny, transparent larvae. These are see-through creatures with small bristly legs and arms. They eat tiny green plants.

As they grow bigger the larvae change colour and become more like their parents.

Where crustaceans live

Most crustaceans, like crabs and lobsters, live in the water, especially the sea. They can breathe through gills or through their skin. Some crustaceans live on land. Woodlice, for example, live in damp wood. Many small crustaceans, such as lice, live as parasites on larger animals.

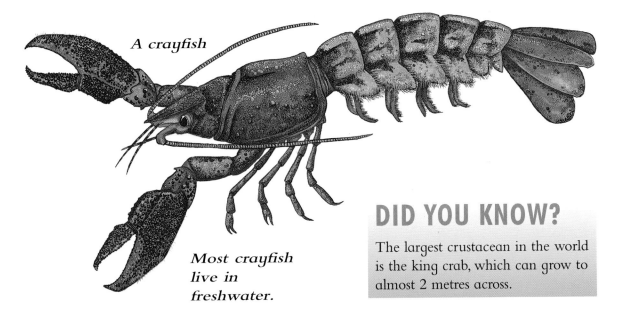

A crayfish

Most crayfish live in freshwater.

DID YOU KNOW?

The largest crustacean in the world is the king crab, which can grow to almost 2 metres across.

Cuba

See also: Island, North America

Cuba is an island in the Caribbean. It is warm and wet. It has beaches and swamps. In the middle of the island are hills and forests.

Living and working

Many Cubans are farmers. Some have small pieces of land for growing food. They keep pigs and goats, and grow coffee. On big farms sugar cane and tobacco are grown. Houses in the countryside are usually built of wood with roofs of palm leaves or corrugated steel.

Street musicians often play rumba music which started in Cuba.

Cuba was once ruled by Spain. In the towns there are still grand old Spanish-style buildings. Music is very popular. Guitar players entertain customers in cafés. People dance to rumba and salsa music.

DID YOU KNOW?

Christopher Columbus probably landed in Cuba in 1492. Spanish settlers started moving to Cuba in 1511.

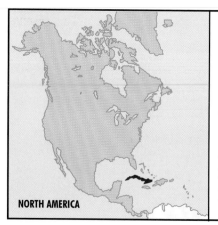

NORTH AMERICA

FACT FILE

PEOPLE......................Cubans
POPULATION...............11 million
MAIN LANGUAGE.........Spanish
CAPITAL CITY..............Havana
MONEY......................Cuban peso
HIGHEST MOUNTAIN....Pico Turquino – 2000 m
LONGEST RIVER............River Cauto – 241 km

Czech Republic

See also: Europe, Slovakia

The Czech Republic is in central Europe. There are mountains and lowlands. Winters are cold and summers are hot. It is wettest in the mountains.

Living and working

Most people live in cities and towns. People work in factories, farms and mines. Farmers grow cereals, root crops, flax and special sweet peppers. The peppers are ground up to make the spice paprika.

A popular meal in the Czech Republic is cheese rolled in breadcrumbs and fried. Meat is usually cooked in a creamy sauce.

The Czech Republic is famous for things made from glass. The Czechs make crystal bowls and glasses, with finely cut patterns. They also make special glass beads.

The ancient capital city, Prague, with its old buildings and large public squares, is very popular with tourists.

DID YOU KNOW?

Before World War I, the name for most of what is now the Czech Republic was Bohemia.

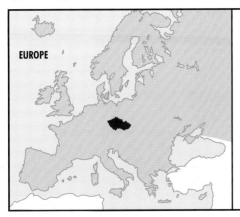

EUROPE

FACT FILE

PEOPLE	Czechs
POPULATION	10.3 million
MAIN LANGUAGES	Czech, Slovak
CAPITAL CITY	Prague
MONEY	Koruna
HIGHEST MOUNTAIN	Hruby Nizky Jeseník – 1492 m
LONGEST RIVER	River Labe – 1136 km

Dance

See also: Ballet, Music

Dancing is moving in time to music or a rhythm. In some dances, such as ballet or Indian kathak dancing, there are very strict rules that control the steps. Other dances have fewer rules. For example, when dancing to pop music, people make movements to fit the music.

These young people are enjoying dancing to pop music.

Dancing around the world

Most countries in the world have their own special dances. Some cultures have special dances for important occasions, such as weddings and harvest-time. Dance is also used in some religions as part of worship or in ceremonies.

DID YOU KNOW?

In some cultures dances are seen as having magical powers. Native American tribes used dances to try and cure sick people or to change the weather.

These kathak dancer must follow very strict rules on how they move and even what expressions they have on their faces.

Day and night

See also: Earth, Season

It is day when the sun has risen and a place is light. At night, the sun has set and it is dark. The earth spins around once every 24 hours, so nearly every part of the world has some hours of light, when it is facing the sun, and some hours of darkness, when it is facing away from the sun.

STAY SAFE!

Human beings do not have eyes that are adapted to see well in the dark. Always wear reflective or light clothing if out walking or cycling at night. Always use cycle lights after dark.

Life at night

People, and most animals, are usually active in the day and sleep at night. Some animals hunt for food at night. They are called nocturnal.

Birds that hunt at night, such as the owl, have eyes that can see by starlight. Other nocturnal animals cannot see very well. They find food using their sense of smell.

Different parts of the earth face the sun at different times of the day. As the earth turns, parts that were light are no longer facing the sun. They become dark. Parts that were dark move into the light as they face the sun.

Animals, like this aardwolf, that look for food at night may have to rely on their special eyesight, good hearing or sense of smell.

DID YOU KNOW?

During winter in the UK days are short and nights are long. At the same time, it is summer in Australia and days are long and nights are short.

Deer

See also: Antelope, Mammal

Deer are large, plant-eating mammals. Deer live in forests, grasslands, swamps and deserts in North and South America, Asia, Europe and North Africa.

Deer families

Male deer are called bucks, stags or bulls. Female deer are called does, hinds or cows. The doe usually has one baby at a time, called a fawn or a calf. Some deer live alone but most live in large groups, called herds. They roam in search of food. Herds of caribou deer walk thousands of kilometres every year to escape the Arctic winter.

DEER FACTS

NUMBER OF KINDS	over 60
COLOUR	brown or tawny
HEIGHT	30 cm–2.3 m
WEIGHT	9–815 kg
STATUS	some types are endangered
LIFE SPAN	10–20 years
ENEMIES	bears, wolves, coyotes, cougars, people

Antlers for fighting

Large ears to listen for danger

Long, thin legs for jumping and running

Hairy coat for keeping warm

A whitetail deer

FOOD

A deer usually feeds at dawn or dusk. At first, a deer hardly chews the leaves, grass and bark it eats. Later it brings a mouthful of food, called a cud, back from its stomach into its mouth to chew again.

The fawn's spotted fur helps the doe hide it from enemies.

Delta

See also: Coast, River

A delta is a piece of low land where a big river flows into the sea. The rivers Nile, Mississippi and Ganges all have large deltas. Not all rivers have deltas.

This is the Mississippi delta, in America. The river divides into many channels as it flows into the sea.

How are deltas made?

As it flows along, a river picks up and carries bits of rock, soil and mud. When the river flows into the sea, it drops all of these things. If the tide does not wash the mud and soil away, it forms a delta. The river divides into many smaller rivers as it flows through its delta dropping the soil. This makes land that looks like the fingers of a hand.

People and deltas

It is very dangerous to live on a delta because of flooding, but farmers like the delta soil because it gives them good crops. This is why people often live on or near deltas.

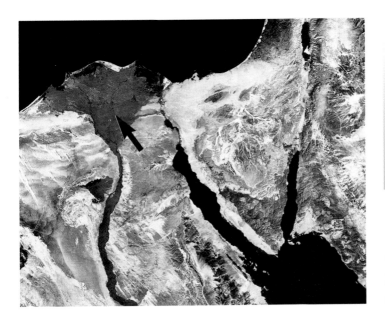

DID YOU KNOW?

The ancient Greek alphabet had a letter called delta, which was written as Δ. Because this is the same shape as the land where the river flows into the sea, the name of this letter was used to describe the delta.

This is the delta of the River Nile in Egypt, seen from a satellite.

Democratic Republic of Congo

See also: Africa

The Democratic Republic of Congo (DRC) is the third biggest country in Africa. It has a very short coastline along the Atlantic Ocean. Half of the country is lowlands, with big winding rivers. There are some mountains in the east. The weather is hot and wet and there are large areas of rainforest.

DID YOU KNOW?

In the Democratic Republic of Congo, there are over 200 different local languages.

Living and working

Most of the people who live in the countryside work on farms. They grow crops such as rice, cassava and bananas. Just under half the people live in towns and cities.

There have been wars in the DRC for many years. This has made it very difficult for people to earn a living and improve their lives.

One group of people in DRC is the pygmy tribe. They are smaller than most other people, and have a very ancient culture.

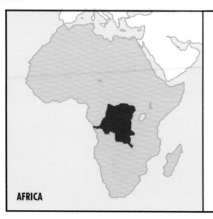

AFRICA

FACT FILE

PEOPLE	Congolese
POPULATION	42.6 million
MAIN LANGUAGES	French and local languages
CAPITAL CITY	Kinshasa
MONEY	Congolese franc
HIGHEST MOUNTAIN	Mount Stanley – 5110 m
LONGEST RIVER	River Congo – 4630 km

Denmark

See also: Europe

Denmark is in north-west Europe. It is mainly lowlands with many islands. The east central area is hilly. Winters are cool and wet. Summers are warm.

Living and working

Most people live in towns or cities. There are many cyclists, so Denmark has plenty of cycle paths. Fish, meat and potatoes are the main foods in Denmark. *Frikadeller* is fried pork meat balls, served with potatoes and red cabbage. *Gravad lax* is salmon and dill, served with a mustard sauce.

Farmers grow cereals, flax, hemp, hops and tobacco. Fish and pork are made into various products. Kaolin, limestone and chalk are mined and made into building materials. Ships, engines and furniture are also made.

The statue of the Little Mermaid, the main character in one of Hans Christian Andersen's fairy tales, is in Copenhagen harbour.

DID YOU KNOW?

Hans Christian Andersen, the famous fairy tale storyteller, was born in Denmark.

EUROPE

FACT FILE

PEOPLE	Danes, Danish
POPULATION	5.2 million
MAIN LANGUAGE	Danish
CAPITAL CITY	Copenhagen
MONEY	Krone
HIGHEST MOUNTAIN	Yding Skovhøj – 173 m
LONGEST RIVER	River Varde-Omme – 145 km

Desert

See also: Cactus, Camel, Climate

A desert is a place that is very dry. It can be hot or cold during the daytime, but most deserts are always cold at night. There are deserts in all continents except Europe. Most deserts are bare rock or sand.

Desert life

Cactus plants can live in hot deserts because they store water in their stems. Wild grass and flowers can also grow quickly in deserts after it rains. An oasis is a place in the desert where there is water. Plants and trees can grow near this water.

Animals such as snakes, scorpions, rats and camels live in hot deserts.

DID YOU KNOW?

The driest place on the whole earth is the Atacama Desert, in Chile.

Not many people live in deserts. Those who live in the Sahara Desert in Africa look after camels and buy and sell other goods.

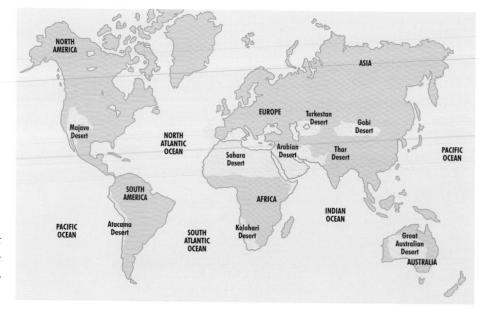

The biggest hot deserts of the world.

Dinosaur

See also: Fossil, Reptile

Dinosaurs are animals that lived millions of years ago. 'Dinosaur' means 'terrible lizard'. There were many different kinds of dinosaur. Some, like the brachiosaurs, were bigger than a house. Some were only the size of chickens.

These scientists are looking for the bones of dinosaurs.

The age of the dinosaurs

Dinosaurs lived on earth for 150 million years. They roamed everywhere. Some dinosaurs, like the tyrannosaurs, were meat-eaters. Others, like the brachiosaurs, only ate plants.

How we know about dinosaurs

Scientists have found fossil dinosaur bones buried in soil, sand and rock. From these bones they can tell what dinosaurs might have looked like, and how they might have lived. They have found out that all dinosaurs hatched from eggs.

What happened?

About 65 million years ago the dinosaurs died out. No one knows why. Some experts think that the climate and temperature on earth changed. Others think there was a great disaster, such as a comet striking the earth. This would have caused dust storms and blocked out light from the sun. Many animals, including the dinosaurs, would have died.

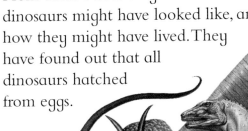

Dinosaurs came in all shapes and sizes.

Dog

See also: Coyote, Mammal, Wolf

A dog is a mammal. Some dogs are trained to work for people, but most are kept as pets. Dingoes, wolves, coyotes and jackals are all members of the dog family, but they are wild.

Dog families

A male dog is known as a dog. A female dog is called a bitch. Young dogs are called puppies. Usually from three to ten puppies are born at a time. A puppy is ready to go to a new owner and a new home when it is about ten weeks old. Wild dogs live in groups, called packs, and look after their puppies in a den.

DOG FACTS

NUMBER OF KINDS	over 330
COLOUR	brown, black, white, blond or a mixture of these
HEIGHT	13–86 cm
WEIGHT	2–96 kg
STATUS	common
LIFE SPAN	usually 10–12 years
ENEMIES	other dogs, people

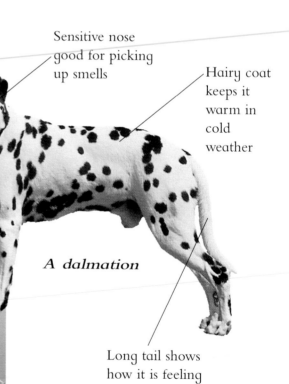

Sensitive nose good for picking up smells

Hairy coat keeps it warm in cold weather

Long tongue for lapping up water

Long tail shows how it is feeling

A dalmation

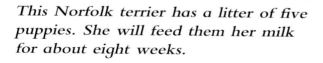

This Norfolk terrier has a litter of five puppies. She will feed them her milk for about eight weeks.

FOOD

A dog eats almost anything, but it particularly likes meat. Wild dogs hunt in packs and chase antelope.

Dolphin

See also: Mammal

A dolphin is a mammal which lives in the sea. The two best-known types are the common dolphin and the bottle-nose dolphin. Dolphins live in all but the coldest oceans and seas.

Air hole for breathing

Beak has teeth to hold slippery fish

DOLPHIN FACTS

NUMBER OF KINDS.... 36

COLOUR..... grey

LENGTH...... 1.7–3.9 m

WEIGHT......70–250 kg

STATUS........common

LIFE SPAN....25–50 years

ENEMIES......Few people hunt dolphins, but thousands die each year, trapped in fishermen's nets.

Dorsal fin help it swim straight

FOOD

Schools of dolphins chase shoals of fish to eat them. Dolphins find their food using sound waves. This is called echo location.

A bottle-nose dolphin

Strong tail fins help it swim fast

A mother bottle-nose dolphin and her calf swim along the sea bottom.

Dolphin families

Male and female dolphins breed and the female gives birth to one calf at a time. A calf can swim as soon as it is born. It stays close to its mother or other females for about one year. Dolphins travel around the sea in groups called schools.

Dominican Republic

See also: Island, North America

The Dominican Republic is a country on part of the island of Hispaniola, in the Caribbean Sea. There are mountains with forests, and flat plains. It is mostly hot and wet, with cooler weather high in the mountains.

Living and working

Over half the people live in towns. Many people work with tourists who go to the Dominican Republic for their holidays.

Every year on Shrove Tuesday there is a carnival with displays and parades. Dominicans dance their national dance, called the *merengue*.

In the countryside there are large farms where sugar cane is grown. In factories, the sugar cane is turned into a sweet brown syrup called molasses.

There are many Spanish-style buildings in the Dominican Republic.

DID YOU KNOW?

Dominicans say that the ashes of the explorer, Christopher Columbus, are buried in the ancient cathedral of Santo Domingo.

NORTH AMERICA

FACT FILE

PEOPLE......................Dominicans

POPULATION...............7.7 million

MAIN LANGUAGE.........Spanish

CAPITAL CITY.............Santo Domingo

MONEY......................Peso

HIGHEST MOUNTAIN... Pico Duarte – 3175 m

LONGEST RIVER.......... Yaque del Norte – 120 km

Dragonfly

See also: Insect

An adult dragonfly is a large insect with gleaming wings. It spends most of its life as a nymph in water, in a pond, lake or river. Then it climbs out and changes into an adult dragonfly with four wings.

DRAGONFLY FACTS

NUMBER OF KINDS	5000
COLOUR	blue, red or green with black, white or yellow patterns
WING-SPAN	up to 16 cm
STATUS	common
LIFE SPAN	up to 5 years
ENEMIES	birds, spiders, other insects, crocodiles

A dragonfly

Large eyes can spot the slightest movement

Spiky legs catch insects as the dragonfly flies

Four large wings for flying faster than most birds

Long, thin body to help it to steer

FOOD

As it flies, a dragonfly makes a basket with its legs to catch smaller flying insects. It holds the insect in its legs or mouth and may eat it as it flies along.

Dragonfly families

A young dragonfly is called a nymph. It hatches from an egg laid in water. The nymph has a thick body and no wings. It feeds on insects, tadpoles and small fish. After one to five years the nymph changes into an adult dragonfly. It lives only for a few weeks or months as an adult.

The dragonfly is in the nymph stage for up to five years. This adult is just emerging.

Drama

See also: Literature

Drama is acting out a story or an idea, usually in front of an audience. Plays, films and television series that tell stories are all types of drama. Drama probably began hundreds of thousands of years ago when people began miming and then adding words to dances.

How drama changed

Drama as it is today began 2000 years ago in Greece and Egypt. As drama changed, people started using scenery, costumes and make-up. This helped the audience to understand the story better. Today, theatre performances, films, videos, television and radio programmes make it possible for many people to enjoy drama.

This scene is from a Greek tragedy. The actors are wearing masks instead of makeup.

This scene is from a film of Shakespeare's play Romeo and Juliet. *It has been filmed many times.*

William Shakespeare (1564–1616)

Shakespeare is the author of some of the most famous plays ever written. His 40 plays, including *Hamlet* and *Romeo and Juliet,* are still performed and studied.

Drug

See also: Human body

A drug is a chemical that acts on our bodies. Medicines are drugs that help us. They can cure diseases or make us feel better.

People and drugs

People have used drugs for thousands of years. Many plants contain natural drugs. Very long ago, wise people knew which ones to give to the sick. Natural drugs are still used, but most drugs are now made in factories. Some drugs, such as cough mixture and aspirin, can be bought in shops. Other drugs can only be bought if a doctor gives you a note, called a prescription.

Drugs can be taken in many ways. Creams can be rubbed on the skin. Pills and syrups can be swallowed. Injections can put drugs into the blood. Gases and sprays can be breathed in.

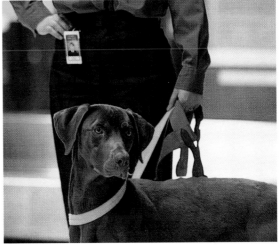

Specially trained 'sniffer' dogs are used to sniff out hidden illegal drugs at airport and ferry terminals.

STAY SAFE!

Children should never take any medicines by themselves. Medicines should only be given to them by an adult they trust.

Illegal and addictive drugs

Some drugs are addictive. If someone starts taking an addictive drug, they want more and more. An addict finds it very hard to stop wanting the drug. Nicotine in cigarettes, and alcohol in drinks, can both be addictive drugs. Heroin and cocaine are illegal, addictive drugs. Illegal drugs are ones that are not allowed by law because they are dangerous.

These pills are being made to help sick people get better.

Duck

See also: Bird

A duck is a bird that lives near water. It has waterproof feathers and webbed feet to help it swim. Ducks can also fly and some can dive. There are many kinds of wild ducks living all over the world. Some ducks are raised on farms. People can eat duck meat and use duck feathers in pillows and duvets.

FOOD

Most ducks eat waterweeds and other plants and insects. Some sea ducks eat fish.

DUCK FACTS

NUMBER OF KINDS...	89
COLOUR....	Most ducks have dull, brownish colouring but some are white and others are very bright.
LENGTH.....	25–75 cm
STATUS	common
LIFE SPAN...	usually up to 10 years
ENEMIES.....	foxes, wolves, bears, large fish, people

Duck families

A male duck is called a drake. A female duck is called a duck. The female lays from four to thirteen eggs in a nest. The ducklings can swim as soon as they hatch. Some ducks migrate in groups called flocks. They fly to warm places for the winter.

A mallard drake

Bill for filtering the water for food

Waterproof feathers for swimming without getting wet

Webbed feet for swimming

A mallard duck and her ducklings swim very close to each other.

Eagle

See also: Bird, Hawk

The eagle is one of the biggest and strongest flying birds in the world. Eagles live in all but the coldest areas. Eagles are called birds of prey because they hunt and kill animals, birds or fish for food.

Eagle families

A male and a female eagle build a nest out of sticks on a rock or in a large tree. The female lays up to three eggs at a time. Usually only one chick grows to full size. The parents feed the chick in the nest for three months. When it starts to fly, a chick is called an eaglet.

EAGLE FACTS

NUMBER OF KINDS	over 100
COLOUR	mostly grey or brown with some white markings
LENGTH	65 cm–1 m
WEIGHT	up to 30 kg
WING SPAN	up to 2 m
STATUS	most are threatened
LIFE SPAN	around 20 years
ENEMIES	People

Hooked beak for tearing up meat

Wide wings and spreading wingtip feathers for flying and soaring

Tail spreads out to help the eagle steer in the air

A tawny eagle

Sharp claws (talons) to kill and carry food

The golden eagle is found in Europe and North America. Only one chick is left in this nest.

FOOD

Different kinds of eagle eat different things. Some eat only fish. Most eat small mammals, birds and reptiles. An eagle can kill and eat animals as big as foxes, or fish as big as salmon.

Ear

See also: Human body, Sound

Ears are used by humans and animals to hear. Parts of the ear also help us to balance.

How the human ear works

The most important parts of the human ear are protected inside the skull. The outer ear catches the sounds and leads them into the ear passage. The sounds hit the eardrum and make it shake. This makes the tiny bones inside the ear, called the hammer, anvil and stirrup, move.

The bones pass the movement caused by the sound along to the cochlea. The cochlea turns these movements into messages that are carried by nerves to the brain. The brain can work out what the sounds are.

EAR FACTS

- Many animals can turn their ears to point towards a sound.
- Elephants have big ears that they can flap to keep themselves cool.
- Some insects, like grasshoppers, have ears in their knees.

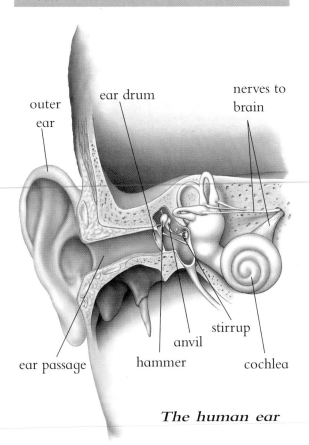

The human ear

DID YOU KNOW?

The hammer, anvil and stirrup are the smallest bones in the human body. All three from one ear would fit onto a thumbnail.

Some animals' ears are specially adapted. The hare has very long sensitive ears so it can run away when it hears enemies.

Earth

See also: Planet, Solar system, Weather

The Earth is our planet. It is one of nine planets that move through space around the sun. The Earth takes one year to travel once around the sun. It is just the right distance from the sun to be warm enough for people, animals and plants to live on, but not so hot that all the water dries up.

What is the Earth made of?

There are oceans and seas over almost three-quarters of the Earth's surface. The rest is land. There is a layer of gases around the Earth, called the atmosphere. All the Earth's weather is in this layer.

Inside the earth

The Earth has an outer skin of hard rock, called the crust. Inside the crust, the Earth is very hot. The mantle is made of hot rocks. The core at the centre is melted metals. Sometimes hot, liquid rock comes to the surface through a volcano.

DID YOU KNOW?

The deepest anyone has gone inside the Earth is only 3.5 km. This is in a mine in South Africa.

From space, Earth is a beautiful, blue planet. Here we are looking down on North and South America.

EARTH FACTS

DISTANCE AROUND THE EQUATOR	.... 40,075 km
DISTANCE FROM THE SURFACE TO THE CENTRE	... 6300 km
TEMPERATURE IN THE EARTH'S CORE	.... 4300°C
DISTANCE OF THE EARTH FROM THE SUN	.... 149.5 million km

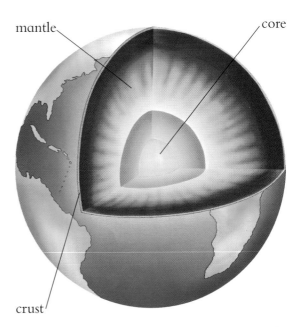

mantle · core · crust

Earthquake

See also: Earth, Volcano

In an earthquake, the ground shakes violently. The land can be split by giant cracks. Buildings can be shaken apart. Earthquakes can cause giant waves called tidal waves.

Why are there earthquakes?

Earthquakes happen when rocks deep inside the earth's crust move. Shock waves spread out like ripples in a pond. The shock waves make the ground shake. Most earthquakes happen along cracks in the Earth's surface.

People and earthquakes

Scientists can measure any movement of the rocks inside the Earth. This helps them work out when there might next be an earthquake. Sometimes, there is no warning at all.

Some parts of the world have more earthquakes than others. California and Alaska in the USA, Iran, Turkey, China, Afghanistan and Japan have all had very bad earthquakes in the last 50 years.

Scientists can measure what is happening in the Earth's crust using measuring machines, like this.

DID YOU KNOW?

In 1906, the city of San Francisco in California, USA was destroyed because of an earthquake. Earthquakes often shake areas of California.

This earthquake happened in California in 1994. It did a lot of damage. Many buildings and roads were destroyed.

Earwig

See also: Insect

An earwig is an insect with two large pincers at the tail end of its body. Earwigs live under stones and in fallen trees all over the world, but particularly in hot countries. Earwigs have wings, but they don't often fly.

EARWIG FACTS

NUMBER OF KINDS....	about 1000
COLOUR....................	brown
LENGTH....................	up to 50 mm
STATUS....................	common
ENEMIES....................	birds, small mammals

Long antennae to touch, smell and feel

Thin back wings folded under the hard front wings

Pincers for holding food and nipping enemies

Hard, shiny covering for protection like a suit of armour

A male earwig

Earwig families

A female earwig lays her eggs in a small hole that she has dug. She looks after the eggs until they hatch. The young earwigs are called nymphs. They look much like adults but without wings. The female stays with them until they can look after themselves.

FOOD

Earwigs feed at night. Earwigs help gardeners by eating snails and caterpillars but they also damage flowers and fruit as they eat.

The female common earwig stays with her eggs as they hatch.

Ecuador

See also: Incas, South America

Ecuador is a country in South America. The high Andes Mountains run through the centre of the country. In the east are the low, hot forests of the Amazon. In the west, along the coast, the land is flat with swamps, deserts and good farm land.

DID YOU KNOW?

Guinea pigs come from the Andes. In Ecuador they are kept for food.

Living and working

Half of Ecuador's people live along the coast. Many work in the large port of Guayaquil. In the mountains, families have small pieces of farmland. Some keep llamas, which are woolly animals with long necks. Llamas are used for wool and meat, and to carry loads.

The Quéchua Indians, some of Ecuador's first people, still live in the Andes. Women wear long colourful skirts, and each village has its own style of hat. The men wear big, loose coats called ponchos.

Many of the native peoples of Ecuador still wear their traditional dress. This family has dressed in their best clothes to go to church.

SOUTH AMERICA

FACT FILE

PEOPLE	Ecuadorians
POPULATION	11.2 million
MAIN LANGUAGES	Spanish, Quéchua
CAPITAL CITY	Quito
LARGEST CITY	Guayaquil
MONEY	Sucre
HIGHEST MOUNTAIN	Chimborazo – 6266 m
LONGEST RIVER	River Guayas – 160 km

Eel

See also: Fish

An eel is a long, thin fish that looks like a snake. Most eels live in shallow seawater, but some live at the bottom of the deepest seas. Other eels live in fresh water.

Eel families

An eel begins life as an egg. A young eel is called an elver. Some elvers float from the Caribbean Sea, across the Atlantic Ocean to the coast of Europe, or up to North America. For ten years they grow and change colour, until they become adult eels. Then some of them return to the Caribbean to produce new eggs.

EEL FACTS

NUMBER OF KINDS	about 600
COLOUR	silver and black
LENGTH	up to 3 m
STATUS	common
LIFE SPAN	about 11 years
ENEMIES	other fish, squid, people

Long fin along the back and tail stops it rolling over

Tail and body wriggles to move along

Gills for breathing underwater

An eel

Fins for steering

FOOD

Eels feed on plankton, fish and animals that live on the seabed. Many deep-sea eels have huge mouths for catching large fish deep down in the ocean.

These young elvers are hiding in an undersea plant.

Egg

See also: Bird

An egg is the female cell of an animal or plant. When it is fertilized by the male, it will grow into a new plant or animal.

Different kinds of eggs

Bird eggs Birds usually lay their eggs in nests. One of the parent birds sits on the eggs to keep them warm. A bird's egg has a hard shell to keep the embryo safe inside, while it is growing. Most of the food for the embryo is in the yolk that surrounds it. As the baby bird grows, it uses up the yolk. When all the food is used up, the baby bird cracks the shell and hatches out.

Reptile and amphibian eggs A female reptile usually buries her eggs. Most reptile eggs have soft shells. Amphibian eggs are laid in water. The eggs don't have shells. They are laid in a protective jelly.

Mammal eggs Mammals, including human beings, also have eggs. A human egg develops inside its mother. It is about the size of a full stop. The eggs of mammals don't have yolk to feed the growing embryo. The embryo gets its food from the mother's body.

EGG FACTS

- An ostrich egg weighs up to 2 kg.
- Cod fish can lay more than a million eggs at once.
- Sea turtles swim thousands of kilometres to lay their eggs on the same beach where they were born.

The hummingbird's egg is very tiny compared to a chicken's egg.

When they are ready to hatch, baby crocodiles break their way out of their shells.

Egypt

See also: Africa,
Egypt (Ancient), Pyramid

Egypt is a country in north-east Africa. Most of the country is desert, except for the land around the River Nile. There are some mountains in the north-east. There is a hot season and a cool season. Cairo, the capital city of Egypt, is the largest city in all of Africa.

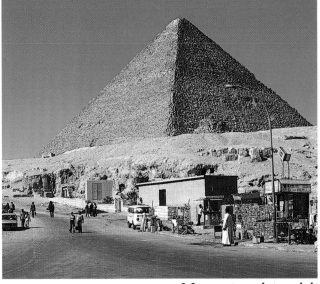

Many tourists visit the pyramids, where the kings of Ancient Egypt were buried.

Living and working

Most people live in the Nile Valley. The flooding of the Nile makes the soil very good for growing crops. The farmers grow date palms, cotton, rice, beans and fruit. Egyptians eat lots of special bean paste called *ful*. It is the Egyptian national dish.

Egypt has many factories. Some of them make clothes using wool from the sheep and cotton that is grown by the side of the Nile. Many tourists visit Egypt to see statues and pyramids from Egypt's ancient past.

DID YOU KNOW?

The Suez Canal is 65 km long. It connects the Mediterranean Sea and the Red Sea. This means that ships can travel from east to west, or from west to east, without having to go all the way round the bottom of Africa.

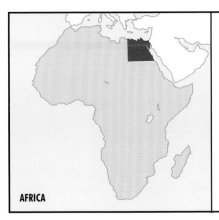

AFRICA

FACT FILE

PEOPLE........................Egyptians
POPULATION...............61.6 million
MAIN LANGUAGES.......Arabic, English, French
CAPITAL CITY..............Cairo
MONEY.......................Egyptian pound
HIGHEST MOUNTAIN... Gebel Katherina – 2637 m
LONGEST RIVER..........River Nile – 6670 km

Egypt, Ancient

See also: Egypt, Hieroglyphics, Pyramid

The Ancient Egyptians lived in Egypt from 3000 BC to 30 BC. They lived in the Nile valley, which flooded each year. When the water went down it left behind mud that was good for growing crops. The rest of Egypt was desert.

What were the Ancient Egyptians like?

Ancient Egypt was very organized. The ruler of Egypt was called the pharaoh. He was in charge of Egypt and its religion. Government officials were also the priests. Most of the people were farmers who grew crops beside the River Nile.

The Ancient Egyptians believed in many gods and goddesses who could bring trouble to Egypt unless they were kept happy. The Egyptians prayed to the gods and goddesses and gave them presents.

What are they famous for?

The Ancient Egyptians are famous for building the pyramids, the tombs in the Valley of the Kings, and for making dead people and pets into mummies. They are also famous for their picture writing, called hieroglyphics.

The Romans took over Egypt in 30 BC. It became part of the Roman Empire.

KEY DATES

3000 BC	The first pharaoh, King Meues, rules Upper and Lower Egypt
2686 BC–2160 BC	The first pyramid is built at Saqqara.
2133 BC–1786 BC	The capital is moved to Thebes.
1567 BC–1085 BC	Many great pharaohs reign, including Hatshepsut, the woman pharaoh, and Ramses II
1085 BC–1030 BC	Temple of Khons is completed.
30 BC	Romans take over

Much of what we know about everyday life in Ancient Egypt comes from studying the painted walls of tombs.

El Salvador

See also: North America

El Salvador is a small country in Central America. Much of the country has mountains and volcanoes, where the climate is cool. There is coast along the Pacific Ocean. Here the climate is warm and wet.

Living and working

People travel across the capital city, San Salvador, in brightly-painted buses. Twice a year in San Salvador there is a parade called the Festival of the Saviour. People carry an ancient religious statue through the streets.

Over half the people in El Salvador live in the countryside. Families grow maize and coffee on small farms. Rice or beans are eaten with most meals. They also eat maize pancakes called tortillas.

Traders, like this fruit seller, pull their barrows down the busy streets.

DID YOU KNOW?

El Salvador had a short war in 1969 with its neighbour, Honduras, over a goal in a football match.

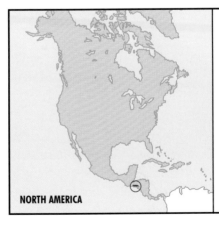

NORTH AMERICA

FACT FILE

PEOPLE	El Salvadorans
POPULATION	5.6 million
MAIN LANGUAGE	Spanish
CAPITAL CITY	San Salvador
MONEY	Colón
HIGHEST MOUNTAIN	Volcán de Santa Ana – 2381 m
LONGEST RIVER	River Lempa – 320 km

Electricity

See also: Energy, Heat, Light

Electricity is a form of energy. It can be used to make things such as motors, heaters and televisions work. Electricity can move along wires or be stored in batteries so that we can carry it around.

How is electricity made?

Electricity is made in power stations. Power lines carry electricity to homes, schools, offices and factories. Some power stations use coal to make electricity. Others use gas, water power, solar power, nuclear power or wind power.

People and electricity

Electricity is clean and easy to use. To use it, people only need to turn on a switch or press a button. Anything that has to be plugged in or needs a battery uses electricity.

ELECTRICITY FIRSTS

1752......Benjamin Franklin (USA 1706–90) experimented with a kite to prove that lightning was electricity

1800......The first batteries were made

1830s.....Generators and electric motors were invented

1880s.....Electric light bulbs were invented by Thomas Edison (USA 1847–1931) and Thomas Swan (England 1828–1914) independently

1890s.....First power stations were set up to provide lights in cities

STAY SAFE!

Electricity can burn and even kill! Never play with plugs or wires! Never go near power lines or transformers!

The energy in the water at the Hoover Dam in the USA is used to make electricity.

Fields of special windmills can be used to collect energy from the wind to make electricity. This wind farm is in California.

Elephant

See also: Mammal

The elephant is the biggest and strongest land animal in the world. Elephants are mammals. There are two kinds of elephants, the Asian elephant and the African elephant.

ELEPHANT FACTS

NUMBER OF KINDS	2
COLOUR	grey–brown
LENGTH	5-6 m
HEIGHT	2.8–3.5 m
WEIGHT	up to 6000 kg
STATUS	Asian elephants are endangered
LIFE SPAN	up to 70 years
ENEMIES	People kill elephants for their tusks.

Big ears flap for keeping cool

Trunk for drinking, bathing, smelling, breathing and picking things up

Tusks for fighting and digging for water

An African elephant

Tail swishes away insects

FOOD

An elephant can eat more than 200 kg of grass and leaves every day and can drink over 120 litres of water at one go.

Elephant families

A male elephant is called a bull and a female elephant is called a cow. A cow elephant has one baby at a time, called a calf. Cows and calves live together in groups, called herds. Bull elephants live on their own.

An African elephant cow, her young calf and her new baby feeding.

Emu

See also: Australia, Bird

The emu is a large bird that does not fly. It is found in the grasslands of Australia. Although it cannot fly, it can run at 40 kph.

Emu families

The emu's nest is built on the ground by the male emu. Up to three female emus may lay eggs in one nest. The male emu sits on the eggs until the chicks hatch. He then feeds and guards them for about five months. When the chicks have grown up, emus move around in small groups. They may walk up to 1000 km each year looking for food.

Short, stubby wings can be lifted up to cool the emu in hot weather

EMU FACTS

NUMBER OF KINDS	1
COLOUR	grey-brown
HEIGHT	up to 1.9 m
WEIGHT	up to 50 kg
STATUS	common
LIFE SPAN	5–10 years
ENEMIES	Farmers shoot emus because they sometimes feed on crops.

An emu

Grey-brown colour helps it hide

Long, strong legs for running fast

FOOD

An emu likes to eat seeds, fruit, and insects. It will also catch small lizards and rodents. It eats quite large pebbles to help grind up the food in its stomach.

These emu eggs are being looked after by a male bird. They will hatch after about eight weeks.

Endangered species

See also: Animal, Plant

An endangered species is a kind of plant or animal that is in danger of becoming extinct. When an animal or plant is extinct, none of that kind of plant or animal is left alive anywhere in the world.

Causes of extinction

Many kinds of plants and animals live only in one sort of place – in the rainforest, for example. If the rainforest is destroyed, the plants and animals have nowhere else to live and die out. Some plants and animals have been collected or hunted by people until there are almost none left.

Some endangered plants and animals are protected by laws. This means that people are not allowed to hunt or collect them. Some endangered animals now live only in zoos and national parks.

The pitcher plant grows in swamps. It is endangered because the swamps are being drained so that people can use the land for factories, farms and houses.

STATUS TERMS FOR PLANTS AND ANIMALS

Some of the plants and animals in the world are very common. Others are almost extinct. This list explains what the different status words used in the animal and plant entries mean:

COMMON .... many found in the species range

RARE .... not often found in the wild

THREATENED ...... fewer than rare, but not yet endangered

ENDANGERED....... so few that it might become extinct

Hunters kill rhinos to get their horns. Poaching has caused the rhino to become endangered.

Energy

See also: Electricity, Heat, Light

Energy gives people and things the power to do work. Everything we do uses energy. Energy comes in different forms. Human beings and animals get their energy from food. The food is the fuel that gives the human or animal the energy to do work. Electricity, light, sound, movement and heat are also types of energy.

How energy changes

Millions of years ago energy from the sun was used by trees. When these died, they fell down and over time turned into coal. Power stations now use coal to make electrical energy. When you switch on a TV set, this electrical energy is turned into heat, light and sound energy.

Storing energy

Some things have energy stored in them. An athlete before a race has the energy to run, but isn't using it. It is stored in the athlete's body. When the athlete starts to run, then the energy is used.

Athletes use the energy stored in their bodies to give them the power to run very fast.

DID YOU KNOW?

When energy is used, some of it is always wasted. Scientists are trying to think of ways to save energy. Insulating houses keeps heat in, and low-energy light bulbs use less energy than normal ones.

Engine

See also: Car, Electricity, Transport

An engine is a machine that uses energy. The energy it uses can be from a fuel, such as petrol, oil or gas. Electricity also may be used to power an engine.

ENGINE FIRSTS

100	First steam-powered toys
1712	First useful steam engine
1875	First petrol engine
1884	First turbine (bladed) engine
1890	First diesel-powered engine
1935	First jet engine
1957	First space rocket

How do engines work?

The way an engine works depends on the kind of energy used to power it. A car engine uses a system called internal combustion. Petrol mixes with air and burns when lit by a spark from a spark plug inside the engine. The hot gases from the burning fuel expand and force parts of the engine to move up and down. This movement is used to turn the wheels.

People and engines

Cars, buses, ships and aeroplanes all have engines. Most of the small machines that people use every day, such as vacuum cleaners and washing machines, have special electric engines called motors. Unfortunately, in most engines the fuel that doesn't burn properly ends up as pollution in the air or water. Even clean electrical engines cause pollution when the electricity is made.

This is a petrol engine in a car.

England

See also: Northern Ireland, Scotland, United Kingdom, Wales

England is part of the United Kingdom (UK). Most of England is lowland or low hills. The highest mountains are in Cumbria in the north-west. There are four seasons, with rain all year round.

Living and working

More people live in London and the south-east than in any other part of England. In the cities there are offices and factories. In the countryside farmers grow crops and raise cattle.

For a day out, people enjoy visiting castles and historic houses, or walking in the countryside. Sports such as football, rugby and cricket are popular.

DID YOU KNOW?

Cheddar cheese was first made in the village of Cheddar, in Somerset, in south-west England.

British police are sometimes called 'bobbies', after Sir Robert Peel who founded the police force.

EUROPE

FACT FILE

PEOPLE	English
POPULATION	46 million
MAIN LANGUAGE	English
CAPITAL CITY	London
MONEY	Pound sterling
HIGHEST MOUNTAIN	Scafell Pike – 978 m
LONGEST RIVER	River Thames – 340 km

Ethiopia

See also: Africa

Ethiopia is in north-east Africa. There are mountains and high, flat countryside. There are also dry lowlands and desert. There is a long and a short rainy season every year.

Living and working

Most people live in villages on the high central part of the country. The traditional village houses are round, with thatched roofs.

The people who live in the countryside grow coffee, cotton, cereals, beans and oil seeds. Coffee is the biggest crop. A lot of coffee from Ethiopia is sold to other countries, but it is also very important to Ethiopians. They have many special customs about how to make and serve coffee.

Ethiopians have traditional ceremonies for serving coffee. This woman is in Gondar Province.

DID YOU KNOW?

Ethiopia had a great drought in the 1980s. Many people died. All over the world, people gave money to help the Ethiopians.

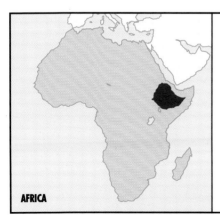

AFRICA

FACT FILE

PEOPLE	Ethiopians
POPULATION	53.4 million
MAIN LANGUAGES	Amharic, English, Arabic
CAPITAL CITY	Addis Ababa
MONEY	Birr
HIGHEST MOUNTAIN	Ras Dashan – 4620 m
LONGEST RIVER	River Abbai – 1370 km

Europe

See also: Continent

Europe is one of the seven continents. In the east, the Ural Mountains divide Europe from Asia. The Mediterranean Sea is between Europe and Africa. The Atlantic Ocean is to the west.

The land

The Alps are the highest mountains in Europe. There are other smaller mountain ranges. The big area of low land through the centre of Europe is called the North European Plain.

Climate, plants and animals

The weather in Europe is wet and cool in the west. It is warmer and drier in the south. Northern Europe has very cold winters. Most of the land in Europe is used for farming. There are still some areas of forest with wild animals, for example, wild deer, mountain goats and wolves.

People and countries

About 728 million people live in Europe. There are about 40 countries, each with its own language and customs. Some of the countries of Europe are members of the European Union, working together to make their countries stronger and richer.

EUROPE FACTS

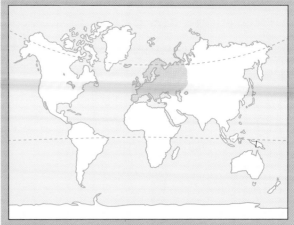

SIZE	10 million square km
HIGHEST MOUNTAIN	Mount Elbrus – 5633 m
LONGEST RIVER	River Volga – 3700 km
SPECIAL FEATURE	The Caspian Sea is the world's biggest lake.

Once every four years, European national football teams play to find the champion of Europe. This is the opening ceremony of the 1996 championships.